CHILDREN OF INDIA

This edition published by Lector House in 2023

ISBN: 978-93-5800-736-7

Lector House LLP
Registered Office: H. No. 96, Block C, Tomar Colony,
Burari, Delhi – 110084, India
info@lectorhouse.com
www.lectorhouse.com

CHILDREN OF INDIA

JANET HARVEY KELMAN

2023

LECTOR HOUSE LLP

A VILLAGE STREET

CHILDREN OF INDIA

BY

JANET HARVEY KELMAN

WITH EIGHT COLOURED ILLUSTRATIONS

CONTENTS

LIST OF ILLUSTRATIONS

CHILDREN OF INDIA

CHAPTER I

THE STORY OF THE WORLD

India is a very old land, and those who live there look far back into the past. They listen to the stories that were told of men and gods in those old days, and follow the customs that were followed then.

There are many gods in India, and many priests who serve in their temples and at their shrines. The priests have more power over the lives of the people than the gods have, but custom has far more power than either gods or priests.

No one can tell how many hundreds of years have passed since the stories that rule the lives of Hindu children to-day were first told. Long before the earliest time of which we know anything in the history of our islands, there were wise thinkers and clever workmen in India, and the men and women of that land think of them and of their customs with awe and reverence. And because much of the life of a Hindu child to-day is the result of the thoughts that have come from that far past time, we must listen to some of those old stories.

Before America was discovered by Columbus men here had strange ideas about the shape of the world. Men in India had thought of that too, long before anyone in Britain did, and this is the picture of the world they made for themselves.

They saw a beautiful large lotus flower held up on the back of an elephant, in the midst of seven seas. One sea was of salt water and another of fresh, and these two were the only ones that were at all like the seas of earth. One of the others was a sticky sea, for the waves that broke on its shores were of sugar-cane juice. Another was clear and sparkling with dancing waves of wine. Then there was an oily sea of melted butter, a flat sea of curds, and a beautiful white sea of milk. But no one had looked at these strange seas, nor had anyone seen the great elephant that held the lotus flower on his back. Only the flower itself at the centre of all was seen or known. India to the south, and the other lands to the north, the east, and the west of the Himalayas, formed the petals of the world lotus, and at its centre amongst the great snow mountains the god Siva sat on his throne on Mount Meru.

ON PILGRIMAGE TO THE MOUNTAIN

There is one special mountain there, to which pilgrims go, and they hold it as sacred as if it really were the ancient Mount Meru. It rises from a grassy plain, and a deep ravine cuts it off from the other mountains. High up it is covered with snow, but towards the foot great cliffs of rock stand out bluish purple against the whiteness, in bands round the mountain. Near the base there is a broad dark band made by a very high cliff, and the priests point this out to pilgrims. "See," they say, "the mark of the ropes of the demon who tried to drag away the throne of Siva."

And the pilgrim gazes with awestruck eyes, for he sees not only the marks of the demon's rope, but also, in the narrower bands higher up the mountain, the coils of the serpent that he has often seen in his images of Siva; and, in the ragged edges of the snow-clad peaks and the icicles that hang from the glaciers, he sees the matted hair of the god. He is tired and weary, for it is months since he left his home in the plains. First he marched through tangled jungle, through grass three times as tall as himself, and under great cane stalks and feathery bamboo trees. In these early stages of his walk he sang and shouted to frighten away the heavy sleepy bear, and to scare the quick-limbed panther that might be resting on any overhanging branch. Then he climbed up through forests of dark cedar and pine, with the white flowers of the magnolia, and the wealth of rhododendrons bright against the dark tree stems. On and on he went into the cold grey passes where his fear of wild beasts was lost in the fear of the spirits of the mountains, and he walked in silence and awe lest avalanche or storm should prove to him their anger. For he felt that he was indeed amongst the homes of the gods. Each moment as he mounted higher new snow-clad peaks rose before him, and those he had already seen seemed higher and greater. His heart was filled with the dream of a rich land somewhere amongst these glittering heights to which his soul might go after death, if only his pilgrimage should win him merit. So, as the sun sent flashes of light across the snowy peaks, the weary man plucked up courage and stepped out more bravely, till at length through a last ravine he saw the hoary head of the mountain he sought, and as he saw it he tore from his threadbare loin-cloth a little rag to tie to a bit of scrub. Other rags hung there, for many pilgrims when they reached that spot had been so poor that they had nothing left to offer at the sacred bush except a bit of the cloth they wore. And so he added another, and left the rags to flutter there in the cold winds of that high land, while he hastened on to finish his pilgrimage, and walk round the sacred mountain.

Other places are sacred besides this mountain that stands for Mount Meru, the centre of the world lotus. Each rock and stream has its spirit, and everywhere amongst the mountains there are shrines and temples and far-off holy places to which pilgrims go in their endless search for rest. Through all the land of India the mountains of the north are held sacred, and often the eyes of men who will never be able to reach them as pilgrims look longingly towards those homes of the gods.

CHAPTER II

THE STORY OF THE GANGES

VERY long ago, though the mountains stood at the world's centre, and India lay at their feet, there was no Ganges river, and the plains lay bare and fruitless. The god Siva then lived on the top of a high mountain, and spent his time in thought. Up over his head above the mountains the Princess Ganga lived free as the wind. She was the daughter of King Himalaya, and the air nymph Menaka, and so her home was in the air among the heights.

At that time there lived a very wise man on earth, and, as he looked at the burning plains of India, and thought of the air princess, he said to himself, "If she would only give up her freedom and become a river, how she could enrich and purify the earth." And when he had thought this out, he began to pray to the god Siva to send Ganga to earth. Siva granted his request, and the Princess floated down to earth. She touched it first at the mountain top where the god sat, but he caught her in the tangled masses of his hair, and for ages she could not escape from them, so the wise man could not see the answer to his prayer. But long long afterwards, she broke away from her prison on the mountain top, and flowed down under the glacier ice, and over the bare grey rocks. She made her way through the ravines, and the great pine woods sprang up as she flowed. Rhododendrons grew on the banks at her coming, and at the foot of the mountains the jungle stretched down to be nourished by her waters. But it was out on the open plain that the Princess Ganga really showed her power. There, fields of wheat and rice and poppies and lentils grew up wherever she flowed, and wherever the streams that joined her from the mountains made their way to reach her. Groups of fruit trees and bamboos grew too, and men came to settle in villages beside them till the plain of the Ganges became a great, bright, busy place with herds of buffaloes watched by little boys, with oxen yoked to the plough, and other oxen carrying the precious river water to pour it on fields that were far from the banks.

But the Ganges is far more than the bringer of food and life to the Hindus, for the sage prayed that the river might flow to bear away the sin of men, and that is a far greater thing than only to bring food. But we must remember that sin means something different to a Hindu child from what we think of as sin. To him it does not mean unkindness, or cruelty, or lying, or even murder; it means breaking the rules of custom.

Because of the sacredness of the Ganges men bathe in it, and pray to die beside it, that after their bodies have been burned on its banks the ashes may be scattered over its waters, and allowed to float away far out to sea. They hope that if that happens, their souls will be lost in the great unknown spirit in which they believe, as the river is lost in the ocean.

Every bend of the Ganges is sacred, and each place where a stream joins it, is yet more holy. Pilgrims go from its mouth to its source and back again. If they walk, they take six months to the pilgrimage, but if they wish to win more merit, they lay themselves down on the ground and cover miles of the bank with their bodies instead of with their feet, and that takes far longer.

There is a great gorge where the Ganges flows out on to the open plain. Near it stands the town of Hardwar, and on the Hindu New Year's day dense crowds of pilgrims gather there in honour of the birthday of the river. They bring the ashes of the dead whom they have loved with them, and as they throw them on the flowing water they feel that they have done for their friends the very greatest thing they could do. Then at a certain moment each pilgrim struggles to be first to bathe in the river.

The most sacred city is Benares, and all the year long its streets and temples and river banks are thronged with pilgrims. They bathe, and throw sandal-wood, sweets and flowers into the river. Some of them wear garlands, and, as they bathe, the garlands rise from their breasts on the water, and float down the current. Then the pilgrims go round the sacred city, a walk of ten miles, and afterwards they offer flowers and gifts in as many temples as possible. After all is done, they turn homewards across the plain, unless they are so old or so ill that they may hope to die soon. If they are, they stay on in the strange city in poverty and pain, for to die in Benares is a better thing to them than to be amongst friends or in the home of their childhood.

But flowers and ashes are not the only gifts that have been offered to the Princess Ganga. Once little living babies were thrown to her waters, and old men and women have been left to her mercy by those who were too heartless or too poor to feed them. These terrible offerings are not seen now, for the British Government has forbidden anyone to throw any living person into the river.

CHAPTER III

THE STORY OF LIFE AND DEATH

Long long ago, the unknown spirit began to play a game of life and death, and he is still playing it. That is what a Hindu child is taught, so life is not a real thing to him, but is only make-believe. Yet the rules of this game are so hard and fast that none of the puppets can escape from them. The Hindu story of life and death all circles round one rule of the game. That rule is that everything anyone does and everything anyone says must be punished or rewarded in another life, so that a little Indian child believes that he has been alive on earth hundreds of times before, and that everything that happens to him in this life happens because of something he has said or done in a life that is gone by, and which he forgets.

He fears too very much to do anything for which he may suffer in another life, for if he does wrong in this life he may be born a woman, or a cow, or a frog, or he may be sent to one of the hells to be tortured by demons there. Because of this, and because, too, the spirits of his gods may be in trees or animals or stones, he is very kind to animals, and he worships trees and stones.

The round of birth and death is very long, for the full number of lives is eight million four hundred thousand, and if, after the soul has made many steps upwards, it breaks a rule of life, it may have to go away back to the beginning.

The one great hope is that some time in the dim future, by keeping all the rules of the game in one life after another, the spirit may be set free from birth and death, and may drop out of the endless game. It may not seem at first such a very terrible thing to go on living one life after another, but the thought of it has become an awful thing to those who believe in it.

Life to them is very hard. Terrible famines come, and bring hunger and plague and death. And men and women lay all that is left to them of food and of money before the gods, and pray them to send rain. Even when there is no famine in the land the daily observances of custom and the weary round of toil depress the spirits of men, so that the more they think of anything beyond the work of the day, the more they long to give up living altogether. A South Indian folksong says:—

"How many births are past, I cannot tell,
How many yet to come no man can say,
But this alone I know, and know full well.
That pain and grief embitter all the way."

Quoted by C. A. Mason *in "Lux Christi."*

CHAPTER IV

THE STORY OF CASTE

FAR back in the early days four kinds of people sprang from Brahma the creator, to form the castes of India. The first, the Brahman caste, sprang from his mouth, to rule all the others. The second sprang from his arms to be the warriors of the land. The third sprang from his loins to be the business men and the land-owners, and from his feet came the fourth to serve the others.

The Brahmans are still the powerful caste. From amongst them priests are taken, and they rule all others. But the other three castes have been broken up into many smaller divisions, till one can scarcely trace the lines that mark the difference between the four that were spoken of long ago. And besides all the castes there are thousands of those who are outside. They are called pariahs, and all the caste men look down on them and scorn them.

In some parts of India those who belong to different castes are as far apart from each other as if the lower caste men were not human beings at all, and a high caste man will not touch a low caste one even to save his life. The Brahmans are treated almost as if they were gods. Many of them live by the gifts of the people, so they do everything they can to strengthen the old customs and beliefs that make the other Hindus worship them. They have strange ways of keeping their power. If a Brahman is angry with anyone he will go and sit on his enemy's doorstep day and night without tasting food or drinking water. Even if the villager does not give in at once, he soon does, because he knows that the Brahman will rather starve to death than leave his door, unless he gets his way, and the poor man thinks of all that may happen to him after death if he allows a priest to die of hunger on his doorstep. He thinks he may go to one of the places of punishment beyond the world, and after hundreds of years come back to earth as a worm or a fly, and so he does what the priest bids him, however hard it is.

It is caste law that tells Hindu children what sin is, and many of its rules are about eating and bathing. No one may eat food with anyone of a lower caste. No one may marry anyone of a different caste. No one may change his religion. There are many rules about what the people of each caste may eat, and how their food must be cooked.

Many of the laws of caste speak of the honour that must be paid to Brahmans, and of the punishments anyone who does not reverence them may suffer. Some of these punishments are so cruel that the government would interfere if anyone tried to enforce them now, but the fear of the pain that may come after death is strong enough to keep very many Hindus still in constant fear of the Brahmans, even though they cannot be punished so brutally in this life as they once might have been. Here are some sentences from the laws about caste.

FAKIRS

"The Brahman is by right the lord of all this creation."

"What being is there superior to him by whose mouth the gods eat oblations?"

"When the Brahman is born he is born above the world, the chief of all creatures, to guard the treasures of religion."

"Thus whatever exists in the universe is all the property of the Brahman."

"No greater wrong is found on earth than killing a Brahman."

"Certainly the king should not slay a Brahman, even if he be occupied in crime of every sort."

"A Brahman may take possession of the goods of the Sudra[1] with perfect ease of mind, for, since nothing at all belongs to this Sudra, as his own, he is one whose property may be taken away by his master. The leavings of food should be given to him, and the old clothes."

"If a man of low birth assault one of the twice-born castes with violent words he ought to have his tongue cut out."

"If he lift up his hand or his staff against him he ought to have his head cut off."

"The dwelling of Chandals[2] and Swapacas[3] should be outside the village; their clothes should be the garments of the dead, and their food should be in broken dishes."

These are only a few out of many, and some of the laws are too cruel to quote here. Yet though all that is written in the old law of India, men have often risen there, who tried to break through the rules of caste, and there are other ancient writings that show that all Hindus have not believed in these differences between man and man.

"Small souls inquire, 'Belongs this man
To our own race, or class, or clan?'
But larger-hearted men embrace
As brothers all the human race."

But those who have held that caste law is not binding have never been able to break the power the priests held over the great masses of the people, and so caste law and not the brotherhood of man still rules.

In many parts of India a boy cannot choose what trade he will follow. If his father belongs to the carpenter caste, he must be a carpenter; if his father is a sweeper, he must be a sweeper; if his father is a robber, he will be a robber. In one place in the far north, when a little boy is born his mother swings him backwards and forwards over a hole in the wall and says to him:—

"Be a thief! be a thief!"

There are castes of robbers and murderers still in India. The caste of the Thugs

[1] Man of low caste.

[2] Outcast races.

[3] Outcast races.

was the most famous one of them all, but now the British Government has taken under its control all those who still belong to it. They are kept in ground set apart for them, and none of them are allowed to go out to kill or to steal.

Yet pilgrims still crowd to the beautiful marble tomb of the man who founded the caste of the Thugs two hundred and fifty years ago. He is one of the saints of India, and the priests who guard his shrine cover the tomb with beautiful cashmere shawls, and lay fresh flowers on it morning by morning.

CHAPTER V

THE STORY OF FATE

WHEN a baby is born in India the lines between the bones of its skull can be traced just as they can be traced in a fair-skinned child. The mother of a white baby does not notice them much, but they mean a great deal to an Indian mother, for an ancient story is told about them.

Very long ago a little daughter was born to Brahma, the creator, and its mother asked the father to tell her what would happen to the little child. Then the god Brahma turned his back to his wife and his baby, and stretched out his hand behind him towards the child. In his hand he held a golden pen, and he wrote with it on the baby's head. He could not see the letters he was writing, but his wife could, and as she read the words she called out to Brahma to change the writing, because she would not have so sad a future for her child. Brahma wrote again, and this time the life he foretold was worse than the first one had been. Again the baby's mother refused to let him leave so cruel a fate on the head of the child, and once more he wrote. But this time Brahma did not give his wife time to speak. Ere she could say anything he threw away his golden pen, and since that day he has only written once for each child that has been born. The future that Brahma writes on the skull is called the "fate," and so each Indian mother believes that everything that will happen to her child is fixed when she first traces on the little skull those curious markings which she calls the writing of the pen of Brahma.

When a baby is born there is great eagerness to know whether it is a boy or a girl. If it is a boy there is joy in the home; everyone is glad, and the mother of the little child at once feels that she has been a good woman, and that the gods are pleased with her because they have given her a son. But if the baby is a girl everyone is sad, and the father if he is asked about it may say, "It is nothing," for he thinks it a sorrow to have a little girl child born. He would far rather have a calf, because a cow is a sacred animal, but the birth of a little girl is a sign of the anger of the gods. Besides that the father knows that he will one day have to pay a great sum to her husband at her marriage. When she is still very young her husband will take her away to his father's house, so that she will never be able to do anything for her father and mother in their old age. So there are many reasons why a little girl is not welcome. She is a sign of the anger of the gods; she will cost a great deal of money, and she will never be able to help her parents.

Sometimes when a father is told that he has a little daughter, he says nothing, but only clasps his thumb round the fingers of his hand, and that is a sign that the wee baby girl is to die. It is very easy to kill a little infant, and where everyone thinks that it is right, it can be done quietly, so that though those in the house know about it, no one will say anything. It is sad to think how many little children are killed in this way still, even before their mother's heart has grown tender to them, but some years ago, before the Government of India set itself to stop this crime, there were hundreds of little baby girls killed openly every year.

And if anyone had asked how fathers and mothers could be so cruel the answer would have been, "It is our custom," or, "It was her fate." For everything depends on fate to the Hindu, and no one can help anything that happens. If an animal is drowned in a well, he leaves it there. It was the creature's fate to fall into the well, and it is not his custom to cleanse the well. The children of the village may sicken and die because of the poison in the well, but that too is fate, and no one pauses to ask whether there may not be some other cause.

CHAPTER VI

THE STORY OF THE PROPHET

THERE are hundreds of other old stories that affect the life of Indian children to-day; but if we remember those which tell us of the holy land—the seats of the gods—amongst the Himalayas; of the sacred river of the Ganges, whose waters are even said to flow underground to feed the other rivers of the land; of what life and death, fate and caste mean to the Hindus, we shall have something to guide us.

But all those who live in India are not Hindus. Once, long ago there was an Arabian named Mohammed. He was a camel-driver in Mecca, but from his early childhood he used to dream strange dreams in which he had visions of angels who came to speak with him. He had a faithful disciple, and he used to tell him what he had heard in his dreams. This man thought the things Mohammed told him were very wonderful, and he wrote them down. He had not books in which he could write them, so he took oyster-shells and bits of wood and stone, and sometimes even the shoulder bone of a sheep, instead of paper, and wrote the teachings of Mohammed on them. Mohammed believed that there was only one God, whom he called "Allah," and he said that he was his prophet. Within his life-time he conquered Syria, Egypt and Persia, and before fifty years had passed after his death his followers had marched through the wild passes of the mountains into India. Since then, there have been many followers of the faith of the prophet there, and whenever they have been strong and powerful they have fought against image worship; indeed one of their great leaders was called the idol-smasher.

The followers of Mohammed believe in fate as firmly as the Hindus do, but in other religious things they differ from them greatly. Their greatest feast day is at the end of the month that they call Ramadan. During the whole month they hold a fast, and eat only after the sun sets. Then on the last night of Ramadan they rejoice not only because the long fast will so soon be broken, but also because it is the night on which they believe their sacred book, the Koran, came down from heaven. But the Koran was really gathered after the prophet's death from the sentences his disciple had written down on the stones and oyster-shells and other odds and ends.

On the morning after this night of gladness all the Mohammedan men and boys gather to the Mosques to praise Allah for the good that they have enjoyed through the past year, and to ask for mercy in the coming one. But sometimes there is not room within the mosque of the city for all who gather to worship, and then those who cannot get into it spread their prayer rugs on the ground under the open sky. Everyone is in good spirits and the beggars know it, and squat on the roadsides ready to call out to every passer-by for gifts. The followers of the prophet are prepared for this and they scatter bread and rice and beans, and handfuls of shells here and there, while the beggars shout and scramble to get as much as they can.

Whenever the service in the Mosque is over, everyone rushes to the shops, where all kinds of Indian foods can be had, for all are hungry and happy. The scene is like a great fair with picnic parties everywhere, only there are no women to be seen. There are old men, and tiny boys; there are farm-servants and wealthy land-owners, but never a lady nor a girl. All day long while the feasting goes on the streets are gay with flowers and banners, and at night fireworks flash out against the dark sky.

It is only once a year that this great feast takes place, but every day the followers of the prophet can be seen at prayer. A call sounds out from the roof of each Mosque, and the Mohammedan when he hears it spreads his rug on the ground by the roadside or in the open field, kneels on it with his face towards Mecca, his holy city, and prays to Allah. When his prayer is done he begins again at his work where he left off, but while the prayer lasts he seems to know nothing, and to see nothing of what is around him, but to think only of Allah and his prayer to him.

CHAPTER VII

CHILDREN IN HINDU HOMES

EVEN in high caste homes, where the women are never allowed to leave their own dingy part of the house, little girls, while they are still very young, play freely with their brothers. They are never thought of with pride as the boys are, and they must keep in the background when a visitor comes, for a father does not like to take any notice of his daughters when a stranger is there, though he will call his boys to speak to his friends. Yet boys and girls together have a happy time. They make mud pies and romp about, and tumble over each other all day long.

Indian boys are very fond of flying kites. Their kites are square, and many of them are different from those we see, in another way, for Indian boys like to make their kites fight with each other, and in order to make the fight keener they draw the strings through a mixture of crushed pieces of glass and starch. After the string is dry, they run off with their kites. If they cannot find a better place, they climb on to the flat roofs of two houses near each other, and send off the kites, and then the fight begins. There are the two kites high up above the trees, a blue one and a green one. The green kite hits the blue, but neither of them is hurt. Then they dodge about in the air for a long time, for each boy is managing his kite well, and it seems as if neither would win, when suddenly the boy of the blue kite gives a sharp pull. His string has caught the string of the green kite and cut it, and the green is dropping to the ground out over the rice field yonder!

There are many curious sights for children to watch in India. One of these is the snake charmer, as he carries his strange pets in a basket or wound round his body. It is not only for his own amusement or for the pleasure of the little crowds that gather round him that the charmer plays. A good Hindu will not kill a snake, nor any other animal. But he is greatly afraid of serpents, so if he sees them near his house, or in his garden, he may send for a charmer to come and play his weird music till the snakes are fascinated, and wriggle to him, and let him shut them up in his basket. When he has carried them away he will take out their poison fangs, and keep them to add to his other pets.

Here is another tamer who has only a sparrow. He carries it safely in the folds of his robe, and when he wishes to show it to anyone he lays it down on the ground. It does not fly away, but hops about till he lays down a heap of beads, which have been hidden in another fold of his garment. Then he holds up a thread in the air. All is ready now, and the bird catches the dangling end, and climbs up the thread and down again. Then the little sparrow lifts the beads one by one, and threads them on to the string. It is all done in the cheeriest way, and the bird seems as happy as the little children who watch him.

A SNAKE-CHARMER

If a boy lives near the jungle he may see the taming of a herd of elephants. First of all he will help to build two great strong fences in the forest. At one end the two fences are quite near each other, but at the other end they are far apart, so that there is a mile or more of jungle ground between them. At the narrow end of the fenced-in ground, there is a large enclosed space, and just where the two fences open into it there is a great scaffolding high up in the air. When all is ready the fence round the enclosure is tested and tried to make sure that it will not give way. Elephants roam the forest in herds, only now and again a lone elephant is found, and he is generally a very fierce one, whom tamers would not wish to capture. After all is ready at the Kheddah,[4] the hunters watch for a fine herd of elephants. When the message comes that there is a herd near, men go out into the forest. They separate and go quietly till they have formed a ring round the herd in every direction, except the one towards the wide opening to the fences. Then when the ring is complete, the men begin to close in towards the herd with shouts. The shouts come to the elephants from every direction except one, and as they seem to hear so many foes they do not know which to attack, and so they rush on wildly in the one direction from which no noise comes. The men close in towards the fences very carefully until the whole herd of elephants is within the wide end of the fenced ground. Each moment the yelling of the beaters seems nearer, and the herd rushes on wildly. Beyond the narrow end of the fences, they see what seems like open ground, and they rush for that. As the last one passes through the narrow space the great scaffolding is allowed to drop, and the elephants are prisoners.

But that is only the beginning of the work, and by far the easiest part. The taming has still to be done. After the herd is captive, tame elephants with riders on their backs tackle the full grown elephants of the herd one by one. Even a strong wild elephant is not a match for two or three tame ones, and the trained ones know their work so well that they soon get the wild creature they are surrounding close to a tree. That is their bit of the work. Then the mahout,[5] who has been on the back of one of the tame elephants, lets himself down to the ground. The tame elephants still keep the wild one close to the tree, and hem him in to keep him from attacking the man who is on the ground, for he is in great danger. He has to slip ropes round the legs of the wild elephant and fasten him to the tree. The first ropes are the most dangerous ones, for when the great beast feels that he is caught, he is desperate, and strikes out in every direction; but the drivers are quick and clever, and soon their prisoner is tied so tightly to the tree that he can do no harm to anyone. Then when he is firmly fixed there, the mahouts try to make friends with him. They bring him fruit and sugar-cane, and all the things he likes best to eat, and they stay by him, talking to him and singing till he grows quite at home with them. Sometimes they can loosen his cords within a fortnight, and lead him off between two others.

There are many other strange sights and sounds in the jungle, and some of them are greatly feared by Indian boys. Though there are many Hindus who will not kill any animal because of their caste rules, there are others who do, and some of them are very clever in catching and killing tigers.

[4] "Kheddah," the name given to the enclosed space.

[5] Elephant driver.

The tiger is a very cruel creature that will kill even when he is not hungry, and if one begins to eat men as well as cattle the villagers live in terror of him. He watches warily by the roadways for any stray passer-by, and he will follow a bullock cart for miles in the hope that some one of those who walk by it will fall behind, and give him the chance of attacking him alone. And so men learn to fear the "pug" marks of the tiger with a terrible fear, and to shudder at the thought of his silent footsteps. When the villagers find that there is a tiger making his lair near their village, and coming to it day after day to steal their cattle or to carry off their children, they first find out where he drinks. That is easily done, for the soft clay near the bank of the river keeps the marks of his paws. Then when they are sure of that, they get three strong nets and hang them from upright bamboos across the path by which he must come to drink. The tiger comes quietly along, and ere he knows he is entangled in one of the nets and has pulled down the first pair of bamboo poles. The more he struggles the more the meshes trouble him, and if he does manage to break through, all trammelled as he is with the broken net, it is only to dash into the next one. There he lies wild and helpless, and struggles till he is worn out. In the evening, the villagers come with their spears and attack the prisoner, but they do not like him to be too quiet. They like him to growl at them, and to try to leap at them. It seems too easy a victory if he is dull and stupid ere they reach him.

The jungle is full of interesting plants and animals, and we could fill a large book with their names and habits, but we must only take time to speak of one other creature. It will form a link for us between jungle sights and sounds, and the splendour of the courts of the olden rulers of which children may still see relics in some parts of India. The animal that links the palace with the jungle is the cheetah, for six cheetahs have been taken from their wild haunts to guard the Uzar Bhagh Palace in Baroda. Through the day they are muzzled, and wander freely in the gardens. They are like small leopards, and they steal about amongst the trees or lie sleeping in the sun through the long hot hours. But each evening they are shut up in the palace. Their muzzles are taken off, and all night long the fierce creatures wander through the passages and halls. For within the closed doors that they guard, the jewels of Baroda, the richest in all India, lie. In the collar of state alone, there are five hundred diamonds, and some of them are as large as walnuts. Round the edge of this collar three bands of emeralds run, and each emerald in the outer row is about an inch square, while a great diamond, that is called the star of the Deccan, hangs down in front. There are many other treasures there besides the wonderful collar, and the most interesting of them are a rug and two pillow covers. The rug is more than ten feet in length and six feet wide, and it and the pillow covers are made of strings of pearls woven together and decorated with diamonds. These jewelled cloths brought the present ruler of Baroda to his throne in a strange way.

Baroda is a native state, whose princes are called Gaikwars. The word Gaikwar means cowherd really, but for hundreds of years it has been the royal title of the rulers of Baroda. These men trace their family far back into the times of the ancient stories, for they believe that they descended from a Hindu hero called Rama, who is now worshipped as a god. This belief strengthened their power, because no one dared to oppose anything that was done by the children of a god, and sometimes they used their power very badly. The British Government tries not to interfere with the Indian rulers, so it honoured this ancient house, and whenever the Gaikwar came to state ceremonies he was received with a salute of twenty-one guns. But though the Government acknowledged the ruler of Baroda, it did not wish cruelty and wrong to go unpunished in the lands it protected, so there was always a representative of the Viceroy in each protected state. During the reign of Malar Rao, the last Gaikwar, Colonel Phayre was the British Representative at Baroda, and while he was there he heard terrible stories of the heartless cruelty of the Indian ruler. He was sure that many of these stories were true, but it was difficult to prove anything against a man who was so powerful.

There was an arena at Baroda where elephants, tigers and lions had fought in former days to amuse the court, and in front of this old arena, Malar Rao built a palace. It was exquisitely finished and very costly, and at the main entrance there were two guns of solid gold, mounted on silver carriages. Not far from the city there was an ancient idol, and at its shrine the Gaikwar built a splendid temple. Those who know about these things say that though it is modern, its workmanship is as wonderful as that of the famous old temples of the land. As Colonel Phayre saw all this, and far, far more, his heart was hot within him, for he knew that the Gaikwar was building all these things with money that he had stolen from his people by taking bribes and by cruel taxes. But the Englishman did not see that he could prevent it, until he heard of the pearl and diamond rug. The jewellers of India searched for three years in order to get the gems that were needed for it and for the pillows, and when at last all were finished the Gaikwar made arrangements to give them as a gift to one of his favourites. When Colonel Phayre heard that the woven jewels, the cost of which had been wrung from the people, were to be given away, he refused to allow it. He said that the jewels belonged to the state of Baroda, and were not Malar Rao's to give.

Now the Gaikwar had set his heart on giving this present to his favourite, and he was so enraged that nothing was too wild for him to attempt. He asked to see Colonel Phayre, and with every show of friendship he invited him to drink his health. The cup of pomola juice was handed to the guest, but an instinctive feeling of suspicion warned the Englishman, and he refused to drink. And it was well, for in the cup there was the dust of diamonds. Once before the Gaikwar had served his end by ground jewel dust. He had killed his brother so, and had ruled in his stead. When he was brought to trial, this and many other things were found out, for his brother was not the only man whom he had killed unjustly.

When he was condemned, the widow of the brother whom he had poisoned was asked to adopt a son, to be the ruler of Baroda, and the boy whom she chose grew up to be a clever and an able man. He has changed the whole life of the state, for he thinks of his people, and seeks to give them many things to make life brighter and easier for them. And as Baroda is called the "garden of India," the children who live there enjoy much of what is happiest in Hindu life. Famine scarcely ever comes there, for the Nerbudda river waters the valley, and the rain clouds that cross the ocean are never spent ere they reach it.

Many children in India now go to schools that are much like our own, but in the far-off villages, the master still sits on the ground, under a broad tree, with his scholars round him. The little boys sway their bodies backwards and forwards as they sing out their lesson, or bend over the sandy ground, to trace the outlines of the Sanskrit letters there as they shout out the names of them after him.

So the days of childhood pass when all goes well, but if illness comes there is terrible suffering. The best that can happen to a Hindu child when he is ill, is to be left alone to get well or to die. If there is something very serious wrong with him, his parents may think there is a devil in the boy, and send for the barber, who does a great many things in an Indian village besides cutting hair and shaving chins. One little boy was getting better after a fever, but though the fever was gone his eyes were still very sore indeed. The barber was sent for, and when he came he did not bathe the sore red eyes, nor do anything to soothe the pain. Instead of that he began to burn the top of the wee boy's black head, to pull the devil out by the burn! So the poor little fellow had to bear the pain of the burn as well as the pain in his eyes, and though the barber's rough treatment was of no use, the father and mother tried no other plan. They let the eyes grow sorer and sorer till the boy was blind, and then they thought that Brahma must have written with his golden pen that their little son would lose his sight. So they did not trouble more about it, but began to think how they could make him earn money. They knew he would never be able to work. So they took him to a large town that he might beg, and make people pity him because of his blindness. But the boy need not have been blind.

Another child called Yogina was very ill indeed. She lay in a fever, and as the fever raged, she said strange wild things, for her mind was wandering, and she did not know what she was saying. The other girls in the house were in terror. They thought some demon had entered into her, and they feared that it might leave her and go into one of them, so a priest who said he could force demons to leave those who were ill was asked to come and cure her.

This man had learned how to say "Am, Im, Um, Em, Aim, Om, Aum, Tam, Tham, Dam, Nam, Pam, Pham, Bam, Mam, Jam, Ram, Lam, Vam, Sam, Ham, Ksh-am," over and over again, each of them in a special tone and way, and that proved to everyone who heard him there that he was a very marvellous man who could do miracles. His name was Mantra Shastri. When he came to the house where little Yogina was lying in her fever, he bade the other women of the house clean out the court, and make a pattern on the wet floor with fine white powder. When this was done, little Yogina was dragged into the court, and set down opposite the white markings on the damp floor. Yogina could not sit up. She was too weak, but Mantra Shastri would do nothing for her if she lay on the ground. So the other women of the house gathered round her and held her up. Then the devil-doctor began his work. He went out and walked round the house several times, and sprinkled evil-smelling water as he went. Yogina cried out louder, for the effort of sitting up made her fever more burning, but all round the house the harsh sounds of tom-toms rose and the child's screams could not be heard. Then Mantra Shastri came into the inner court again, and the women walked in a circle carrying trays of fruit and flowers and leaves and rice. The tom-toms still beat on, and their noise only made the sick girl wilder. She did not know anything of what was going on around her, but she fought blindly with those who tried to hold her up.

The priest took little heaps of rice from the trays the women carried, and set them down in front of Yogina amongst the white marks on the floor. One heap was of white rice, one of yellow, and one of black, and when he had laid them there he spoke to the demon in the sick girl and said:—

"Oh Spirit of Evil, where do you come from? What do you want?" The women who were round Yogina were so eager to hear what she would say, that they forgot to hold her up, and she fell forward on the rice.

Even when they raised her she had no answer for the priests' question. At last he seized a cane, and beat her to make her speak, and as the blows fell on Yogina's back she started up and ran twice round the court. Then she fell. A shout rose from everyone there, for they believed that the evil spirit had left her at last. But it was life that had left her, and the little child, who might so easily have been nursed back to health, had been killed.

That is one story of one little girl, but it is not unlike many, many others that might be told, not only of girls, but of boys and men and women, who die because there is no one who knows how to nurse them, or to help them to get well. And many who do not die are ill all their lives afterwards, because of the way in which they have been treated.

CHAPTER VIII

BOYS AND GIRLS

But the children of India have to act as men and women long before anyone here would think them old enough to do more than learn and play. Very early indeed a little Hindu child is married. Sometimes a baby is married in the cradle, but a little girl is generally nine or ten years old before she goes away to her husband's house. That does not mean that she and the little boy to whom she is married have a cottage, and live there together. It only means that she comes in, a frightened wee girl, to a houseful of people whom she never saw before. The oldest woman in the house takes charge of everything. Often she is the grandmother of the child's husband, and the little wife must not only do everything the old grandmother tells her, she must try to please all the other women there too, if she wishes to be happy. If she makes the others like her, and if the boy to whom she is married likes her, she may soon be as happy there as she was at home, but if she does not get on well with the others, there is no one who can save her from misery.

One bright little girl called Runabai left her father's house to go to her husband when she was eleven years old. Her father had been sorry when she was born, but she was so loving and happy that everyone had grown very fond of her, and she went away with beautiful Saris[6] and many flashing jewels. Her father was a wealthy man, so he sent twelve maids with his little daughter to wait on her, and keep everything about her as nice as it had been when she still stayed in his house. But her husband's family did not like her. They took away all her beautiful clothes and jewels, and instead of letting her twelve maids wait on her, they made her work very hard herself, and do much more than she had strength for.

Then before a year had passed they began to starve her. She was only allowed to eat once a day, and then all the food she was allowed to have was rice and red peppers. One day she was cleaning the house, and she saw a little piece of bread on the table. She was hungry, and she was only twelve years old, so she picked it up and began to eat it. But before she had time to swallow a mouthful her mother-in-law caught her. She took the bread and pushed it down the little girl's throat with a stick.

Little Runabai was sometimes allowed to go home to see her people. One time she begged them to keep her with them, and not to allow her to go back to the terrible life she had to lead. Her father was very sad. The tears were in his eyes, but he was afraid of the disgrace it would be to his family if he kept her from her

[6] Woman's garments.

husband. He knew that his caste would be broken if he did. So in spite of his sorrow he said, "Go back, and if you die it will be honourable." She did go back, and in two months she did die, and her father and mother mourned for her, but they comforted themselves with the thought that she had died honourably!

But though a Hindu wife is often free from the pain and misery that killed this one, there is always a great fear that hangs over her, for her husband may die, and then she will be a widow. If a little wife dies, her husband may marry again, but a high caste Hindu widow must never marry a second time. Often little girls are married to full grown men; sometimes, even, they are married to old men, so it very often happens that a girl becomes a widow when she is only a child, and there are Hindu widows who are not one year old. At first the child may not know that there is any change in her life, but as she begins to grow older she finds that all the hard work is left for her, and that no one wishes to see her when a feast or a wedding is held, or when anything bright is going on. Then one day a priest comes to her village, and to the house where she lives. She is not afraid of him, for she knows no reason why he should be angry with her. But he is angry with her. He says her beautiful black hair must be cut off, and soon the barber comes and shaves her head all over. After that time she is only allowed to eat one meal a day, and twice a month she does not even get that one meal. She has to wear a rough Sari that lets everyone know that she is a widow even if she covers up her little close-shaved head, and in some cases she only has that one dress for night wear and day wear till it is so ragged that it will scarcely hold together.

Besides all that, the friends of her husband think that they cannot be too cruel to her, because they believe that she must have done something very wrong indeed in one of the lives she lived long before, and that it is because of that, that she is a widow. They think that if their boy had married another wife he would still be well and bright.

But though girls suffer far more from the early marriages of India than boys do, the boys have to bear many unnecessary burdens because of them. They have to work hard in order to help to get food for the household, and wee boys labour for long days in the rice fields. They guide the oxen at the plough, and they carry the pots of water from rivers and canals to fill the little channels that water the fields; and sometimes, even with all these early years of toil, a young man finds that he cannot feed his family or give gifts to the gods. Then he goes to a money-lender, and if he once does that, there is little happiness for him or for his children, for the money-lender will take everything from him, his jewels, his wife's jewels, her clothes, all but the plainest which she keeps to wear; and then perhaps his fields will have to go too, and the cruel money-lender will send men to watch the rice, and the millet, and the wheat as they grow, for fear any of the crop should be reaped without his knowledge.

But before a Hindu boy marries he has been taught how he must worship the gods. A little Brahman boy puts on the sacred thread which marks his caste, and which he wears over his right shoulder, when he is eight or nine years old; from that time onwards he must keep all the rules of his caste. When the thread is first put on a priest whispers into the boy's ear the sacred text or "mantra" of his family. He must remember it well, for he will have to repeat it over and over again each morning before bathing and then again each evening. He must always repeat his text and bathe before he tastes food. If he is a good boy, he will say his text over and over again very often. In some parts of India he must not stop until he has said it one hundred and eight times.

The sacred thread is not the only mark by which a boy shows his caste or the god he worships. He may have a white V marked on his forehead, or a yellow W, or a wavy line right across, with perhaps a grain of rice stuck in the centre, and if he is going to a feast he will have a bright red dot there too.

Hindu boys repeat the names of their gods as well as the sacred text of their caste. One little boy who wished to be very careful that he worshipped his gods well used to say, "Rama, Rama, Rama," until he had said the name twelve thousand, five hundred times; and then he said, "Siva, Siva, Siva," six thousand, two hundred and fifty times, every day.

There are special days and weeks at each shrine and temple, when there is more merit in offering gifts than at other times, and on these days people throng to lay their presents before the gods. They bring oil or camphor for the priest to burn in a censer which has a large lamp in the centre for the camphor and five small ones round it for the oil, and when the priest lights the lamps he waves the censer before the idol, and the sweet scent of the camphor fills the shrine. Others bring melted butter and rice, and others fruit and flowers. Marigolds are the favourite flowers to bring, and the temple steps are strewn with them. But with all the other offerings there must be, if possible, a little money, for the priest will look eagerly to see if there are any pice[7] in the offering.

There is no place to which larger crowds of people go to worship than Benares, and if a boy is lucky enough to be there he will see many curious sights. He might see these things in other cities too, but not so many of them all together.

The strangest people he will see are the Fakirs. They wander about from city to city and from temple to temple, and live entirely on the gifts that are given to them by the devout. Even if a Hindu does not wish to be kind and generous, he will give a gift to a Fakir, because he believes that if the Fakir curses him his rice will wither on its stem, his cattle and his children will sicken and die, and ill-luck will follow him in everything. So the very shadow of a Fakir is held sacred, and no one will cross it lest harm should come to him for his want of reverence.

The Fakir wears as little clothes as possible, but he covers his body with mud and ashes, and makes his hair stick out in all sorts of uncouth forms with gum and clay. He wears a rope or some strings of beads round his neck. Sometimes he whitewashes his face, and paints lines on it, and makes himself still more uncanny-looking than he already is with his thin body and his wild hair. He has a boy whom he calls his "Chela" with him, and a brass bowl, and nothing else. The boy goes out with the bowl at breakfast time, and begs till it is full; then he comes back to the Fakir where he rests on the temple steps, or under a cart, or by the wayside, to eat the meal with him. The Fakir himself should never beg, for the gods he wor-

[7] Very small coins.

ships are supposed to send him all he needs, and if he receives nothing from them, he must starve. Some Fakirs are earnest men who seek to live up to the best they know, and some are only idle loafers who wish to have an easy life, and to get as much as they can by trading on the hopes and fears of other people.

A WAYSIDE SHRINE

Amongst them there are many men who have wonderful powers of conjuring and of second sight. No one can explain the tricks they do, and there is a weirdness about the men that adds to the weirdness of their doings. Many an English child would run home in terror at the mere sight of a Fakir. But the sight of a Fakir is not nearly so eerie as the sight of some of the things he seems to do. One of these men will suddenly appear to climb up into the air going hand over hand on a rope that is not there, till he vanishes into the sky. In a few minutes he will come quietly along the street as if nothing had happened. Another will take a piece of rope, whirl it round his head, and toss it into the air, where it will seem to the onlookers to stand so firm and strong that a man can climb it, though it is not fastened to anything. One of the commonest of these wonderful things is to make a plant grow while the crowd watch. The Fakir takes a mango fruit, opens it, and lifts out the seeds. He has a little tub of earth into which he drops them, and as the bystanders watch, they see a mango tree grow up, and bear fruit before them.

The chela sees these things, and gradually learns the secrets that belong to them, so that when his Fakir dies he is ready to take his place and be a Fakir himself.

The ways in which the gods are worshipped vary greatly. Some of the idols are washed and dressed and fed each morning, and bathed and put to bed each night, and there are long rites that are performed in the temples. But, there are also many wayside shrines where men and women lay their offerings as they pass, and murmur a few words of prayer.

Often a new idol is found. For the Hindus think that the spirit of a god may enter an animal or a stone or a tree as the spirit of a man may enter any one of these.

One day a Brahman priest lay in a temple court, drowsy and troubled. The reason of his trouble was that plague was in the city and the people fled from it, and the offerings that were brought to the temple were poor and small. The priest was full of dread alike of the plague and of the poverty that would face him, if the gifts to the temple grew less and less. Soon the drowsiness grew stronger than his anxious thoughts, and he fell asleep. As he slept he dreamt that a great goddess appeared to him, and told him that she had come to the city in a block of stone, but that she had not been worshipped, and so she was angry with the people, and had sent the plague, and that if honour were not done to her she would send fire to finish the work that plague had begun. She wished the people of the place to hold a feast, and then to carry the stone in which she lived away hundreds of miles over the country to Benares.

The priest wakened, and, as he thought of his dream, he remembered a great block of black marble that lay beside a temple that had just been built in the city. Ere the women came to gather round him that day after offering their gifts in his temple, the priest had thought out the meaning of his dream, and he told it to them, as they gazed in awe and fear. He said that the stone in which the goddess dwelt should have been polished, and set up to guard the entrance to the new temple; but the workmen had not seen that the stone was a special one, and had left it aside, and the goddess in her anger had burned up the fields. The women sighed, for this part of the story was only too true. The fields were hard and bare, because there had been no rain, and the river beds were dry. Plague had followed famine, and death was at the door. But the priest told of more terrible things yet, for he said that Mariamma, the angry goddess, would send fire if she were not honoured speedily.

The story of the priest was soon known throughout the city, for each one told it to another. Within a few days fire broke out in the palace of the Maharajah there. The fire as it raged and destroyed the beautiful building made everyone sure of the truth of the priest's vision, and hurried plans were made to have the goddess in the stone carried one stage towards Benares.

The people thronged round the marble block. The new temple stood near, but all eyes were on the stone, not on the temple. Then the priests began their work. They washed the stone all over with milk lest anything might have soiled it while it lay untended. Then they brought cocoa nuts and limes to lay before it. After that it was wreathed with garlands and painted with saffron, and lamps were swung backwards and forwards which filled the night air with the scent of burning camphor.

The crowd watched eagerly, and when the great stone with its added weight of flowers was lifted on to the shoulders of eight men, their joy burst out in shouts, for did they not know that famine and plague and death would leave their city with the goddess.

Music and lights marked the great procession as it wound its way through the narrow darkened streets. Without the city gate eight men waited to carry the idol forward. Many of those who had followed it through the streets turned back, but some pressed on to see the stone pass into the hands of new bearers at the next village. There the lights, the music, and the gaily decked stone struck awe into the minds of the village-folk, and they fell in worship before the block, and hastened to find men to bear it on. So the black marble block travelled over many miles of the land. It never reached Benares, for a priest on the way dreamt another dream about it. He dreamt that Mariamma wished to rest in his village, so he had a shrine built for her; and there, amidst lamps and garlands, the unused stone received the worship of the people from the country round, and the priest grew wealthy by the gifts that were brought to the goddess in the marble. But the other priest, Ramachandra, died of the plague which he had said would leave the city with the angry goddess.

Some Hindu gods look very terrible. One of these that is commonly worshipped is called Ganesa, and he has a man's body with an elephant's head. Whenever a Hindu is going to begin a new piece of work, or to do something important, he makes offerings to Ganesa, for he believes that the elephant-headed god can take obstacles out of the way and give success.

There was a little boy in Madras called Ramaswami, who went to worship Ganesa for the first time. As he trotted down through the bazaar by his mother's side he chatted gaily. He had garlands on his arms, and his hands were full of incense. He had listened to his mother when she told him how to lay his gifts in the god's lap, and when to bow to the god, but he was not thinking much about the god or the gifts.

The temple was a small place, as Hindu temples often are, for crowds of people do not worship in them together. One by one, or in small groups, they bring their gifts, offer them to the idol, and turn away.

The doors of this temple were wide open, and Ganesa sat in the gloom inside, right opposite the entrance. The boy saw a black figure as large as a man on the back of a great stone rat. The eyes, the tusks and the red mouth of the elephant-head gleamed out of the darkness, and the trunk was lifted up at one side, as if it would strike anyone who came near.

Ramaswami screamed with terror, and hid behind one of the pillars from the dreadful god. His mother had grown used to the appearance of the idol, and she only laughed at her wee boy for his fear. She pulled him from his hiding-place, but before she could drag him to Ganesa he had slipped from her grasp, and had run wildly down the street. When she saw that he was gone she hurried after him, and when she caught him she was breathless and cross. She pushed him back before her and said, "You little fool. Is your father's son going to be a coward? The god will not strike you. Don't you see he is made of stone and cannot move?" At last Ramaswami stood close before Ganesa, but his terror was still as great as ever. He threw down the garlands and the incense, but he forgot all his mother had told him of the way in which to give them, and the movements of worship to make before the idol, and when his hands were at length empty of the offerings he wriggled once more from his mother, and fled as if the elephant-headed god was at his heels.

But all Hindu boys are not frightened of the idols. There seem always to have been those who wished something greater to worship than a stone, and who could not believe that any good would come of senseless offerings. One of these was called Chikka. His home was in a village in Mysore, and one day a friend came to it with an image of Lakshmi, the goddess of fortune, and asked Chikka's father to take care of the idol for him. Not long after that Chikka's father found that he must leave the village. He did not wish to carry Lakshmi with him, so he laid her carefully in a box, and gave her to the village priest that he might take care of her. Misfortune came to the friend who had left the idol, and he began to fear that it was because he had not been worshipping the goddess, so he hurried to the village to which Chikka and his father had gone, and said to the boy, "Come along with me, and we will fetch Lakshmi here and worship her together." Chikka was only ten years old then, but he had thought out some things for himself, and he said, "The goddess Lakshmi has left us poor, while you are rich. When she gives us good fortune we will worship her, but not till then." His father was angry when he heard what Chikka had said, but his anger did not have any effect on the boy, for only a year later he did a far more daring thing. He and his brothers and sisters were ill, and a fortune-teller was called in to say what the parents should do to make them well. This man said that the reason of the illness was that no one in the house had been worshipping serpents. So two old stone serpent idols were brought out and consecrated. But though the others did honour to them Chikka would not.

He watched for a time when no one was beside to interfere with him, and then he broke the stone snakes into pieces and threw the fragments away. When his father found out what had been done he was extremely angry. He was frightened too, for he thought that some terrible harm would come to them all because Chikka had insulted the idols. But in a few days the children were well again, and no other hurtful thing had happened to them, so Chikka won his parents over to his side, and they ceased to believe in the serpent god.

CHAPTER IX

THE KING OF INDIA

ONCE upon a time a boy was born in a manger in Bethlehem. When He was still a child wise men from the East came to worship and to lay gifts before Him, because they had seen a star which guided them to His cradle, and they knew that He was born to be a King. The wise men worshipped the child and returned to their homes in the East, and the child grew up to be a man. And when He had reached the full age of a man He went about in His own land, and taught and healed the sick, and there gathered around Him a band of men who walked through the fields and villages with Him. And as they walked with Him, it came to be known among them that this man was no other than the Son of God, that He had come to live on earth to save mankind from sin, and that He was indeed the ruler of all the peoples of the world. By and by wicked men put Him to death on the Cross, and those who had walked with Him were in deep sadness. But on the third day they saw Him again, and they were glad, because they knew now that He was greater than death; and they knew, what they had only guessed before, that He was indeed God. These men thought that their own nation was cared for by God more than others, but after their Master had withdrawn Himself from their sight, He taught them that all the world is beloved of God, and that in each land He must reign. So it came to pass that as these early followers of the King wandered hither and thither, when they came to countries that they had never seen before, they said each to the other, the men of these lands too are the servants of the King, though they do not know Him; let us tell them of His nobleness, and of the glory of His kingdom. In this manner the subjects of the King grew rapidly in number, and they came to be called Christians, because of the name of Christ, or Saviour, by which they spoke often of their King. At that time there was much commerce between the nations of the East, and great caravans with the rich wealth of India came to the places in which the Christians dwelt. And when men saw all these riches, they said let us also go there, that we may heap up to ourselves gems and gold. So it came to pass that families of Jews and of Persians bade farewell to the friends and neighbours of their youth, took the long journey across the desert, and made their home on the hot shores of India. And amongst the families who went there, there were some who had owned the Child of Bethlehem as their King, and because those who truly know Him find Him so good a King that they wish all men to serve Him, these early settlers spoke of Him to those with whom they met, and they won many of the simple folk of India. But the hot airs of the Indian valleys, and the strange faiths and fears of the peoples there, closed in on the little bands of Christians. They still named Him their King, but they did not any longer obey the laws of His kingdom, so the strange worship they saw around them had power to lessen their first eagerness. Down through the years they have owned the name of Christ, but much of the spirit of His kingdom has been lost.

But elsewhere the subjects of the new King pressed forward. And ever when they remembered that He had conquered death, and was a living monarch whom they must obey, they did great deeds to bring in the kingdom that He had bidden them win for Him. Hundreds of years passed on, and the countries of Europe all owned the reign of the Son of God in name, though many of the people there thought but little of obeying His laws. The commerce of India no longer came to Europe chiefly by the hot desert routes. Great ships sailed from the ports of Europe to harbours in India; and Spain, Portugal, Holland, France, Germany, Denmark and England each held possessions on the shores of India that had been given to them by those who ruled the greater part of the country—the warlike followers of the prophet.

And so, because these nations held land in India, their people spoke often of the men and women who dwelt in it, and of their trade and wealth. And the stories of travellers were heard with wonder round the fires of northern Europe, and under the sunny skies of Spain.

Now though there were many Europeans who cared for nothing except to get as much ease and comfort for themselves as they could, and who would not give up anything for the kingdom of Christ, there were many others who thought much of that kingdom; and when they heard that a new bit of land had been given to their country on the Coromandel Coast or on the Malabar Coast, they longed to know that the people who dwelt in it had been won for Christ. And when they heard stories of the cruel and dark deeds that were done to please the idols there, they longed to have the worshippers know that the real King of the world is served by good deeds, not by bad ones. And so as these thoughts grew amongst them, Christ the King came once more to earth, and laid His Commission on men and on women, and said to them, as He had said long ago to other followers, "Go ye into all the world, and lo I am with you alway." Thus men went from Germany and from England and from Scotland and from America, and at this day the army of Christ's followers in India, who have gone there from other countries, is great and strong, and throughout the land the tokens of the kingdom that is to be, can be seen to-day. There are churches where Indian men and women, who have welcomed their King, meet to worship Him. There are colleges where boys and girls can learn of the greatness of His work in the world. There are hospitals and leper homes, where the followers of Him who healed the sick in Galilee labour to heal and help some of the sore sickness of India. And still more real beginnings of His kingdom are seen in the lives of the men and women and the boys and girls who have found Him and loved Him.

But though Christ is the King of India, those who own His sway there are only very very few, and He still needs those who love His thoughts and His kingdom in other lands to help to carry His message more and more into the heart of India.

CHAPTER X

NEW SIGHTS IN INDIA

MEN and women have gone to India to tell of the King of the world, and because of that new things are coming into the lives of the children there. There is great excitement when a European is seen for the first time in an Indian village. One day the boys of Holapura heard that an English lady had entered the house of the headman of the place. They left their games and hurried to the hut, but ere they got there, it was crowded to the door, so they climbed on the roof and looked down through the holes in the thatch. As they looked in they saw the crowded room and the white lady. A woman was bringing out a blanket from a dark inner room, and was spreading it on a mound of earth, which did for a seat, and now the white lady sat down and the boys gazed and listened. They saw a streamlet of water trickling across the mud floor at her feet; they saw the little room packed with women and boys and babies, and in amongst them they saw the household cow, the goats, and some chickens; but these things did not astonish the boys at all; they had often seen a crowded hut before, and even when Ruthamma, an Indian Christian teacher who was with the white missionary, began to speak, they scarcely listened, for all their attention was fixed on the stranger. But they began to listen a little when she sang "What a friend we have in Jesus" in their own language. Before many lines had been sung a goat made up its mind to go out, and there was so much bustle amongst the children about his going that Ruthamma had to stop and begin her hymn over again. The boys listened eagerly, till suddenly they heard a swoop and a whiz through the air. They shrank back, for vultures are not nice birds, and this one was coming very near. It shot past them through the hole in the thatch into the room. A dead fowl hung from the roof. The bird clutched it and flew away again. The fowl was gone; everyone rushed out and shouted to make the vulture drop it. But the bird would not, and when it had flown far far away from the village, the little group gathered again. But this had spent much time, and Ruth hurried on in spite of a lively quarrel between two wee boys, who, when their grandmother tried to catch them, vanished underneath the cow, to sit and make faces at each other there, and be quite ready to begin to fight again when the missionaries had gone.

That is how some children first hear of the King of India. But of course they understand little of what they hear for a long time. Sometimes the children catch up the tunes and the words of the new songs, so unlike their old ones, and remember them. In a town far from this village, a missionary was riding along the street one day, when he heard a sound that seemed familiar. He checked his horse and looked and listened. No one in the side street noticed him. There he saw a little Hindu boy with Hindu men and women around him. He was singing away heartily in Telugu:—

"Jesus loves me, this I know,
For the Bible tells me so!"

When the verse was finished a Hindu asked him:—

"Little fellow, where did you learn that song?"

"Over at the school."

"Who is Jesus, and what is the Bible?"

"Oh, the Bible is the book sent from God, they say, to teach us how to get to heaven; and Jesus is the name of the divine Redeemer that came into the world to save us from sins: that is what the missionaries say."

"Well, the song is a nice one anyhow; come sing us some more."

But it is not only when words are spoken or sung that the traces of the King are seen in India. One of the most important things that happens there is the digging of a well, and here are some boys who are talking excitedly about a new well in their village. Let us hear what they are saying:—

"Yes, truly they got water—beautiful clear water, and it rushed in so fast that the men who dug had to flee for their lives."

"And yet they did not have a Brahman to bless it?"

"No, I have told you they follow Christ. They do not obey the Brahmans."

"Tell us what they did."

"It was the time of heat! The river was dried up, and the new buildings of the Christians were almost finished. But as it was not fitting that this new religion should find shelter in our village, our priests had tried to prevent them from getting land. They did not succeed in that, but they forbade the Christian people to drink from the wells of the village, and behold the river was dry. The face of Raghu, the leader of the Christian folk, was sad, for what can man do without water? But he went away to consult the foreign teacher. When he returned, he was no longer sad, and it began to be said in the village that the Christians would dig a well within their own ground. Many heads were shaken, for no one thought that water could be found there. When the Christians began to dig everyone was still more amazed, for they did not dig at the lower end where water might soon be reached, if it were to be found anywhere, but high up, close to the dwellings of the low caste men. It was at the edge of their ground, and we all gathered to watch; each man had some taunt to fling at the foreigners, for they did not do anything to appease the gods; they did not consult with the wise men, nor call the priests to bless the well; they made no offerings at the temple, nor did they feast the Brahmans; and everyone was certain that no water would be found. It is true they did pray to their own God, but everyone was sure He had not given them good guidance, for a child may know that a well should not be dug near the dwellings of outcasts.

But in answer to all the Christians said only, 'We will surely get water.' And they believed this, for they worked on day after day through the great heat until the well was so deep that they had to dig through rock—soft rock it was, it is true, but still hard enough to break the points of pickaxes. Weeks went on, and we ceased to watch the well of the foreigners, or to taunt them. It was an old story in the village, but when at any time we passed near it we could see that the digging was well and rightly done, and that if only water had been there, it would indeed have been a great well. But one day, as the village shops were quiet in the heat, there came a cry down the street, and the sound was of men who called, 'We've got water.' But we would not believe it till we ran to the well. There, as we bent over, we saw depths of water, beautiful clear water. The God of the foreign people had given them water! Come and see the 'Jesus Christ well,' and you will know that I tell the truth."

Another boy was bitten by a deadly snake. He was much surprised when he was bitten. He had gone out with his uncle to work in the fields. All through the sugar-cane fields there are channels for water, and if anything falls into these channels to stop the water from flowing through them the sugar-cane will not grow. Timmaya Reddi was pushing along the bank of a channel, bending aside the tall cane stems to make way for himself, when he saw that the flow of the water was checked by something that he thought was a stick. He struck at it with his hook, and as he struck, the reddish-brown stick sprang up, for it was a deadly serpent. Timmaya leapt back, but not in time to save himself. The serpent bit his ankle, and then glided off into the canes. The poison was swift and powerful, and the boy fell back and remembered nothing until he awoke and opened his eyes under a tree beside the white doctor's tent. Timmaya did not know what had happened. He had not felt his uncle lift him and run with him to his mother's house, and lay him there as if he were dead. He had not heard the death wail rise from the village, nor had he heard the rush and clamour when a Christian shouted, "The missionary doctor! Take the boy to him. He came last night. He is in his tent now. It is only a mile away by the short cut."

Thus the noise went on, but the boy was unconscious of it all. Strong men carried him by turns, down a steep path into a valley, up the other side through bushes and then on, over the fields, till they reached the white doctor's tent.

But when they laid him down, it seemed to everyone there too late, and they said that he was dead already. One man alone thought there was time still. He was the doctor, who sternly bade the eager crowd be silent while he fought for the life of the boy. And he won. In half an hour Timmaya opened his eyes and asked, "Where am I," and in two days he walked back across the valley to the village where the death wail had arisen for him.

There is another sad time at which many Hindu boys catch their first glimpses of the King and His followers. It is the time of famine. One night a little boy lay awake, gazing out at the sky through an opening in the house. He watched the heavy clouds break and scatter, and as the stars shone out, they brought sadness to him, not joy, for they meant that the clouds had broken and gone, and that one more night must pass without rain. As he lay he heard the sound of the priests chanting the prayer for rain at the temple, and every now and then the chant was broken by the clanging of bells that rang out on the still air. The boy thought of his father, who was spending the night there at the temple praying for rain. Then he thought of the long days of famine, and of how old his father looked; and he remembered how little that father had eaten during those days of famine, and how much he had always tried to leave to his mother and his brothers and sisters. And so the boy passed a restless night, and wondered what could come to change these awful days of famine.

Then in the early morning he heard his father's step, and as it came to the door a wail sounded from his mother within. His brother was dead. The long misery of famine had been too much, and the eldest son in the little home had died. The next days passed in a dream to the boy. He knew that his father could no longer bear the pain of watching his children die, one by one, and he heard him say that he had made up his mind to seek the nearest relief camp. He remembered that he was lifted into a passing bullock cart along with his mother and three other children, and that his father trudged beside them. The driver of the bullock cart had been a wealthy man, but his servants were gone, and he was leading the ox to a patch of prickly pear, the only green thing that was left in the whole famine land. But the bullock was as weak as the men, and the sun was high ere they reached the patch of prickly pear. They all ate the leaves greedily, and would scarcely wait to pluck out the thorns. Then he remembered lying under the bullock cart with his mother and the other children, and watching his father and the bullock driver disappear in the distance, and he remembered no more until he lay in the clean white shed that had been quickly built to be a hospital for the famine children. His sisters and brothers were there with him, but help had come too late to save the lives of his father and mother.

In these and countless other ways, the new kingdom of love is seen in India, and can be judged even by those who do not own Christ as King. But there are many who do own Him, and find how much He has to give besides the healing of bodily ills. You remember Chikka, who broke the serpent idol? He was one of the first who learned to serve Christ, though he had to wait a long time before he heard of Him. Chikka's family was poor, so he could not go to school, nor learn to read or write, and for many years he had no one to tell him of any god other than the idols he despised. He was nearly forty years old before he heard of Jesus Christ, and after he had learned about Him, he saw that He could do for him all that the gods of stone could never do. Soon he and the missionaries urged the people of his village to give up worshipping idols. The villagers had seen that no harm had come to Chikka, and they began to think that perhaps it was really true, as the missionaries said, that it was the worshippers that kept the god Runga safe in his temple, and not the idol that kept them safe. They left the god alone to see if he could take care of himself. They brought him no fresh flowers, nor did they see that there was oil in the lamp that burned before him. Very soon the garlands withered, and the lamp went out. The temple became dirty and untidy, and worst of all, the roof fell in just over the god's head. But though the villagers gave up the worship of the idol, that did not mean that they were willing to become Christians. At Chikka's baptism, they took sudden fright lest drops of water should fall on them by mistake, and make them Christians against their will, and they rushed out of the church till they blocked up the door, and some of them had to climb out by the window.

RESCUED FAMINE CHILDREN

CHAPTER XI

ANANTA, THE SEEKER

THERE have often been learned Hindu men who have lost their faith in idols, and the story of one of these has so much to do with the lives of many children in India to-day, that we must not miss it out.

Ananta Shastri was a seeker for the King of India, though he did not know it; and his daughter Ramabai is now helping hundreds of little girls to find Him.

Many Hindus think that no woman ought to be allowed to learn to read or to write, or to study the sacred books. Even if a husband is a learned man, he cannot talk much to his wife about the things that interest him, because she would not know what he meant.

Ananta Shastri was a very able man, and he did not think that it was a good plan to keep girls ignorant, but it was not easy for one man to do much to change this custom of the Hindus. One day, as he was travelling, he met another Brahman. The second man had a little daughter, nine years of age, with him, whose name was Lakshmibai, and before the two Brahmans parted they had arranged that Ananta would take the child home with him to be his wife.

The marriage day is generally a very gay one, and sometimes the brightness and the excitement help to make the little wife forget that she will have to leave her own home, and all those whom she has loved, and go away with a stranger, to be under the rule of her mother-in-law or aunts-in-law. But there were no marriage gaieties for Lakshmibai. She was handed over to Ananta, and went away with him, and she never saw her father or mother again. But though the case seemed a very hard one, her lot was really much better than a child wife's often is, even when all sorts of gaieties and feasting take place, for Ananta was very kind to her, and took her carefully home to his mother, that she might teach her all the duties of a wife, and show her how to cook and to grind. When the daily work was done, Ananta wished to teach his wife to read and write. He tried again and again, but his own people always interfered, till he saw that it would be impossible for Lakshmibai to learn if she stayed in his father's home. Many a man would have given in, but he would not give in. He went away from his home, and took his little wife with him far into the forest. There was no sign of the life of man where they rested during the first night. The little child lay in terror on the ground. All the stories she had ever heard of wild beasts and spirits came back to her, and it did not need memory to bring fear to her heart, for right across a ravine a tiger roared and prowled. Ananta watched by her through the long night. Soon he built a hut to be a home for them.

Though Lakshmibai had not been long with her mother-in-law, she had learned all that she needed to know for the simple out-of-doors life. Now her other lessons began in earnest. She was a clever child, and Ananta found great joy in teaching her. The beauty of the old Indian poems seemed doubly great as he recited them to his wife, or listened to her repetitions of them. The days passed swiftly into years. Disciples gathered round Ananta, and soon a little dark-haired daughter was born and then a son. Both of them were taught along with the band of disciples just as if they had both been boys. Then another little baby girl was born into the home, but by this time, Ananta was so busy with the older two and with his disciples that he had no time to teach the baby Ramabai, and all her early lessons were given to her by her mother. But Lakshmibai too was busy. She had to fetch water, to cook, and to bake, and the only time at which she could be free to teach her little girl was when the faint light of the morning stole through the tree stems to the door of the forest-dwelling. Then Ramabai was wakened and lifted from her bed, and she learned all her earliest lessons in the dim morning light from her mother's lips.

Sanskrit is not now spoken by any of those who live in India, but all who know Indian scholarship know it. It was in this language that Ramabai learned the beautiful Hindu poems, and the stories of the gods. There is much in these poems and in the stories that is ugly and bad, but we can feel sure that it was the most lovely parts that were taught to the child in the wood.

When Ramabai grew older she joined the others in their studies, and then her father found to his great delight that this youngest of his children had a mind that could answer to his own in no ordinary way.

By and by the time came when the eldest daughter must be married. Ananta was a Brahman, and he would have been disgraced amongst all his people if he had not married his daughter while she was still a child, so she had been betrothed to a Brahman boy when she was very young. When this took place, Ananta arranged that the little boy was to be educated as she had been, so that the two might have many thoughts and interests in common. The wedding day came, and Ananta sought to have everything as beautiful and costly as custom demanded for the marriage of his daughter, but his heart was bitter within him, because he found that the promises that had been made to him about his son-in-law had all been broken, and he knew that he had given his daughter to one who could not understand her. And this was not his only reason for sorrow. Custom had made him give her a large dowry, and spend great sums of money on the marriage feasting. Brahmans and beggars had been fed too, and he found that he had left himself and his children poor. This made him feel more strongly than ever that there was much that was wrong in Hindu customs. He lectured on the wrongs of India's women, and tried to prove that many of the things they suffered were not commanded in the old writings. But another trouble was before them. Ananta could not face the thought of giving Ramabai to the same fate that had awaited her sister. So he resolved that he would not marry her to anyone until she was grown up. His friends and relations had been very angry with him for teaching his wife, but they had not made him an outcast for that, but when they saw that he was not going to arrange for Ramabai's marriage, they were enraged, and would not own him as one of them. Then came the years of a great famine. None of Ananta's people would give him work, and no one had money to pay for listening to lectures, so the little family moved about from place to place. They always hoped that the gifts they had given to the gods would bring them favour sooner or later. But one misfortune followed another until at last they resolved to die. Ananta had ceased to worship idols, but he had never heard of Christ. Yet, though he had not heard of Him he was feeling his way as many a Hindu has done, towards that same God whom Christ has revealed. Yet though this is so, it did not seem to him that it would be wrong for him to kill himself, for he believed as his fathers had done in the worthlessness and wretchedness of human life, and that belief made him think it right to leave it. The family talked in sorrow and bitterness, and planned how they each in turn would end the life that had become so sad. But the training that Ananta had given to his children, and the close bonds of love that had been drawn amongst the forests, were stirring instincts that he did not dream of. It was a terrible thing to Hindu minds for a Brahman to do labourer's work, but Ananta's son felt that it was a far more terrible thing to see the father whom he honoured take away his own life, and the lad made up his mind that he would find work of some kind no matter how humble it was, and so bring food and life to his father and mother.

But though they were saved the pain of knowing that their father had taken his own life, they could not keep him with them much longer. The suffering and want of these days of weary travel had told on him, and with anxious thoughts about the future of his children, he died. Amongst his last words was a special message to Ramabai that she should always obey and serve God, for though the family still worshipped idols yet Ananta had come to believe that there was only one God in the universe, and that He would take care of those who obeyed Him.

Caste and custom with their grim shadows watched over Ananta's funeral. He had put himself outside the bonds of caste, and no one would help to bury him. At length the sad rites were over, but Lakshmibai was so ill that her children feared that they would lose her too. They could not find steady work even of the humblest kind, and the one thing open to them still, they could not do. They could not beg. The spirit of Lakshmibai was broken. She could fight no longer. There was no refuge to which she could be taken. If she had killed both of her baby daughters, doors might still have been open to her amongst her caste people and relations, for the mother of a son, even when she is a widow, is not wholly despised; but because, instead of killing Ramabai, she and Ananta had taught her and had refused to have her married when she was still a child, every door was shut against her. There was no hospital nor home to which she could go. For many a sick man and woman in India the only hospital has been the waters of the Ganges or a living grave. It was terrible for Ramabai to see the suffering of her mother, and one day she started out to beg—only she could not do it when she came to the point. But the woman to whose house she went saw the little pinched face and the hungry eyes, and gave her a bit of bread with which she rushed home to her mother, who was by that time too weak to eat it, and very soon Ramabai and her brother were left alone in the world.

CHAPTER XII

THE PANDITA RAMABAI

RAMABAI and her brother were alone, but they had one treasure that very few Hindu brothers and sisters then had. They had their friendship for each other, their common interests and hopes and fears.

They were still very reverent to shrines and idols, though strange thoughts and questions were rising in their minds, and the thought of the one great God of whom their father had spoken to them grew ever stronger. One day they found that they were near a sacred lake, in which there were seven floating mountains;—at least they were called mountains, but they were really only small hills. On the shore of the lake there were priests, for worship was paid to the spirits of the mountains. Ramabai and her brother had often heard of this spirit-haunted lake, for it was a place of pilgrimage, and the wonderful thing about it was that if the pilgrim who prayed at the water's edge was good the mountains slowly moved towards the shore, but if he was bad the cliffs remained stolidly still, and no prayers could move them one inch. When Ramabai and her brother reached the lake they found that what had been called mountains were only wooded island mounds, but there they were, all seven of them, rising from the still waters.

The priests warned everyone who came that they must on no account bathe in the waters of the lake because of the crocodiles. They seemed to be so much afraid that any of the pilgrims might be eaten up, that they kept a very strict watch all round the lake.

Ramabai and her brother knelt by the shore. They had been true worshippers of the gods, and they felt that if they were to be judged by the best of the old books of India they were good. It is true that their caste-fellows had disowned them, but, though many of their old beliefs about idols and shrines still lingered with them, they did not believe that a good god could be angry at their father's treatment of his daughters. So they worshipped eagerly, and looked to see if the mountains were moving to the shore. But the water lapped against the banks as calmly as before, and not an extra ripple could be seen. They slept that night near the lake, and very early in the morning, before the priests were on the watch, the boy made up his mind that if the mountains would not come to him he would go to the mountains! Ramabai watched him breathlessly, for had he not the anger of the spirits to dread, as well as the hungry crocodiles? He swam out to the nearest mountain, swam right round it, and back to the shore. No crocodile had touched him, and the look in his eyes as he returned to Ramabai was a look of anger, not of fear. He had seen, when he reached it, that the mountain was only a sham. It was cleverly built of mud and earth, on a floating raft. Trees and creepers were stuck into the clay as if they grew there. Behind, out of sight of land, there was a little boat. It was all clear to him now. Some signal must pass from the priests on shore to the priest in the boat, and if the pilgrim gave enough of money to the priest on shore, the boatman pushed the floating mountain towards the land; so it was not virtue but money that moved the spirit of the mountain. This discovery opened their eyes to many other things. If the worship of the gods was only kept up in order to give money to the priests; and if, in order to keep up this great system, the priests had to call to their aid the gloomy spirits of caste and custom, then there might be escape for India from these terrible things. And with eyes open to all she saw, Ramabai began to notice more than ever before what a terrible life high caste Hindu widows had to live when they were not the mothers of sons. Gradually she and her brother gathered groups of people to listen to them as their father had done. Soon the days of poverty were over, for Ramabai had found out where one of her great powers lay. Crowds gathered to hear her speak, and to wonder at her knowledge. But this relief came too late for her brother, who had been so much worn out with want that his strength gave way, and though he saw his sister safe from the fear of poverty it was very hard for him to leave her alone. But though Ramabai's faith in idols had gone, her faith in God grew stronger through the years, and she cheered the dying boy with the words, "God will take care of me."

Ere her brother's death the fame of Ramabai had come to the ears of the learned men of Calcutta, and they asked her to come and meet with them. They questioned her, and listened to her answers, and they sat in amazement as they heard her quote the ancient writings. They were so moved by her learning that they gave her the right to use the title Pandita,[8] which no woman had ever been allowed to use, and they called her also Sarasvati, "goddess of wisdom."

About this time a Hindu gentleman, whose ideas were like those of Ananta, and who shared Ramabai's horror when he thought of the life of many Hindu women, asked Ramabai to be his wife, and very soon after her brother's death she was married to him. They were very happy together, but they were not content to be happy alone. They dreamed and planned what they could do for Hindu widows, and they even thought of opening their own happy home to them. Soon a little daughter was born to them to add to their gladness, and the plans for the widows were going forward brightly, when death crossed the threshold, and Ramabai was left a widow—a widow with no son. But the shadows of caste and custom had already wreaked much of their vengeance on her, and now when she might have suffered most severely, she was nearly out of their power.

Her whole thoughts were for Manorama, her little daughter, and for Hindu widows, and her one desire was to be fit to do the best for them she could. English women lived in happiness with their brothers and friends. English people had opened schools and colleges in India, and she resolved to cross the sea that she might learn from them in their own land, things that would help her to brighten the lives of Indian women. So the young Hindu widow with her little baby came

[8] Feminine of Pandit, teacher.

to England. At Wantage the wonder of Christ broke on her, and she saw that the God in whom she had blindly trusted was He who had been shown to men in the life and death of Jesus Christ. As Ramabai saw how great a difference this made to her, her thoughts went out to the memory of her father, and she answered his last words as she could not when he died, "Yes, I will serve Him always."

A SCHOOL FOR GIRLS

To-day Ramabai is surrounded by children. She has two homes, and they are quite different. When she gave up her life to Christ the first great piece of work she did in service to Him made many people think that she was not faithful to Him, because in her first home, a home for Hindu widows, the great shadows of caste and custom are admitted. Perhaps at first it seems wonderful that this should be. But as Ramabai looked round the land she saw that many other servants of Jesus Christ had opened homes for high caste Hindu widows, and that no inch of the door of these homes was open for caste and custom. She saw too that only very few Hindus were willing to let their daughters learn from those who would not allow them to follow caste rules. So she made up her mind that she would open one home to which little Hindu child widows might come, although they still sat in the shadow. At first very few were allowed to come, but soon the number grew greater. The little ones were taught many things and they were kindly cared for, and none of their many customs were interfered with. They were allowed to go to the bazaar to buy offerings to carry to the gods, and to have the barber shave them in his rounds. They might fast when they wished, and they need never hear of the faith of Jesus Christ. Ramabai did all that she could to rob the shadows that lay on them of their darkness, only she did not say that they must leave the shadows before they came to her. But ever as the children lived in the Sharada Sadan, they saw that there was one woman—a Hindu widow—on whom the shadow did not rest, one room in which there was no gloom. The woman was Ramabai, and the room was hers. Night and morning she held service there with her servants and Manorama, and the door of the room was always open. It is not easy for shadows to linger round a glowing light. Ramabai knew that, and she waited and hoped. She did not wait in vain, for soon her pupils began to wonder what it was that made her so different from others, and they came to ask her about Jesus Christ and His religion.

Some of the little girls who came to her had been terribly ill-used, and often it was a long time before she could bring a smile to the dim eyes that had lost their childlike look, or even before she could bring health back to the beaten, burned bodies that sometimes came into her loving care.

It was difficult for Ramabai to get hold of those who needed her help most. One time she heard of a little widow who was in great misery, but the child was so stupefied with pain that she did not wish for relief from it, or think that anyone could help her. Ramabai asked the girl and the relations of her dead husband to come and visit her, in order that she might win the love of the young widow, and persuade her to stay when the others went. The relations were glad to visit Ramabai, and they stayed for some time in a little house within the grounds of the Sharada Sadan. Ramabai hoped that the care the child received while she stayed there would have an effect on her, and that before her relations left the place the widow would be eager to stay. But the days went on, and the child was still lifeless and dull, for though the Pandita did not know it, her relations managed to beat and ill-use her every day. At last Ramabai felt that she could wait no longer, so she told her guests in what was understood as the correct way, that their visit had come to an end. Then she asked the widow if she would stay behind. The relations did not wish her to stay, but they could not prevent her if she said she would, and she did say so, though she was still so dazed that Ramabai feared she would lose her after all. On that life the early years of pain have left traces that will never entirely go away.

When Ramabai had carried on her work in this school for eight years, a famine broke out in Central India. She read of this famine, and the thought of all the orphans who were left friendless by it moved her, so that she hurried off to the famine district, and brought back with her three hundred girls. The pupils of the Sharada Sadan welcomed the little waifs, and made room for them within the grounds for that night.

Some time before this the Pundita had bought a farm in order to provide for her widows' school. The famine children were taken to this farm and nursed back to health there. Though in the Sharada Sadan Ramabai led the girls to Christ by indirect means only, she did not feel that she was bound to do so in the farm home. The famine orphans were a gift to her from God, not a loan from parents or relations, so she has from the first been free to tell them of the love of Christ the King, for all children, and for all in sorrow. The new home is called "Mukti," that is "Salvation," and high up over the great entrance the words "Praise the Lord" in Marathi, tell of Ramabai's wish to call the walls of her children's home "Salvation" and its gates "Praise."

CHAPTER XIII

HORMASDJI PESTONJI

BEFORE we leave India we shall hear the stories of four others of its children who found their way to Christ the King. The name of the first of these is Hormasdji Pestonji. He was not a Hindu, nor a Mohammedan, but a Parsee. There are not very many Parsees in the world, and most of them live in India. They are a powerful people, though they are few in number. Their religion is a worship of fire, and their ideals of character are high and noble.

Hormasdji went to a mission college in Bombay. Though no one had to be a Christian in order to study there, yet each one had to listen to lessons on the Christian faith, and to take his turn in reading the Bible. Many of the boys hated the foreigner's religion. They went to the classes because they wished to learn English, but they would gladly have closed their ears when the Bible lesson came. Hormasdji was one of the fiercest of these. When he saw the name of Jesus he refused to say it, and he tried to destroy the books in which it was. But he could not help hearing.

Parsee women are not treated as most Mohammedan and Hindu women are. They are honoured and loved, and may go in and out with freedom; and home life amongst the Parsees is often bright and happy. Hormasdji was extremely fond of his mother, and she died when he was still very young. He was in passionate grief as he saw her body carried out, covered with rich shawls, to the great white towers of silence by the sea, where the Parsee dead are laid. "O god Fire give me back my mother, give me back my mother," he prayed; but his brother came sadly back without the body he had borne away, and the boys were motherless.

Hormasdji thought of his prayer, and began to wonder if 'fire' really was God at all. His lessons at school made him wonder still more, for there were strange experiments with fire and with water, and it did not seem to him that what he had seen with his eyes could be true if fire was really God. He became very unhappy. He did not wish to believe that Christ could be anything to him and he had lost all faith in his own god Fire.

One day he went for a swim in the sea. Before he plunged in he saw a sandbank on which he often rested, clearly marked, but while he was swimming the rising tide covered the bank and there was no resting-place for him anywhere. He turned back to swim to the shore, but it was too far away and he felt his strength failing. As his strokes grew feebler he thought of Christ and everything seemed different to him from what he had imagined. He knew that in his heart he did believe in Christ though he had tried to think that he hated Him. Those on shore saw that Hormasdji was in danger and set out to rescue him, but he did not forget the thoughts that had passed through his mind when he seemed to be sinking. It was in a different spirit that he listened to the missionaries afterwards. He was not content to hear only what was taught in school. He wished to know all he could about the King of India, so he went to the house of a Christian who lived in Bombay. He met another Parsee there, who also studied in the college. It was a joy to them both, for neither had known that the other wished to follow Christ. From that day onwards they stood together, shoulder to shoulder. When Hormasdji was nineteen years old, he was baptised, four days after his friend. All Bombay was excited. No one had ever left the Parsee faith before, and the Parsees stirred up the Hindus and both together tried to kill the young converts. When a trial at law was brought on, some of the Parsees clung to the wheels of the carriage in which Hormasdji drove away from the court and said that they would willingly die themselves in order to kill the man who had left their faith. They tried to poison him and to set fire to his house but all in vain. Hormasdji remained firm and spent his long life, for he was seventy-one when he died, in seeking to bring the faith of Christ into other hearts.

CHAPTER XIV

SITA THE WIDOW

Sita was only a child but she was very miserable. The other little girls she knew romped and played about, but she had to work hard and to bear blows and many other kinds of cruelty. She did not know why this was, but she could remember a time long before—at least it seemed long before—when people were kind to her, and she could play and romp about too. Even in her dim memory of these days one person had been unkind to her. An old man who had shaken her and told her to be quick and grow up that she might work for him. But one day he died, and Sita was very glad. Only she was not allowed to be glad long, for the others in the house came round her and told her that she had killed him, and from that time they ill-treated her terribly. She had to draw and carry all the water that was needed for washing and cooking; and a great deal was required, for there were nine people in the house. Sometimes she was terribly tired, and it seemed as if she could not draw up one bucketful more of water. One day, when she was ten years old, she was more tired than ever, and she sat down for a little by the well, while happy careless women drew up their bucketfuls and put them gaily on their heads. They looked bright in their cotton robes, and their hearts were bright too for they sang little songs as they clustered round the well. Sita thought there was a kind look in the face of one woman who came, and she said to her, "Will you not draw a little water for me, the well is so deep, and I am tired and ill?"

The woman started back from the little brown figure with the tattered clothes and the shaven head. "Widow!" she said. Then she cursed Sita and told her that she had done her harm by letting her shadow fall on her, and that she would have to take a bath before she could eat; and then she cursed her again.

The child looked up in surprise. She did not know what all this meant. The tears were in her eyes, and the woman, with a touch of pity, stopped a moment, when she was safely out of reach of Sita's shadow, and asked:—

"Why should I help you when the gods have cursed you? See, you are a widow." But Sita only gazed at her.

"Don't you understand? Did you not have a husband once?" "Yes, I think so, the old bad man who used to shake me." "You call him bad?" "No wonder the gods hate you. You must have been very bad once. So now you are a widow, and by and bye you will be a toad or a snake." Then the woman lifted her water-pots and hurried away.

Sita hastened too for she knew she had stayed too long, and when she reached the house she was so tired that she nearly fell, but instead of a cool drink or kind words her sister-in-law burned her arms and hands with a hot poker because she did not go to work quickly enough and the little one had to labour on through all her pain.

So the days passed one by one. Some were worse and some were better. But Sita was always hungry for since her head was shaved she was only allowed to eat once a day and that only of the least pleasant kind of food. She was lonely too, for most of the children fled from her. But there was one girl called Tungi, who used to manage to speak to her sometimes. Tungi was a little wife, but she had not yet gone to stay with her husband. He was in school, and he had sent word that his wife must go to school too, till they were both older, because he wished her to be able to sing and to read books and be happy with him when he spoke of the things he cared about.

Tungi's mother did not like this at all. She thought as very many people in India think that it is a bad thing for women to read and write; but Tungi was married, and, just as her mother would not have thought it right to save her from her husband if he had been ill-using her, so she did not think it right to refuse to let her go to school.

Tungi was a bright girl and she quickly took in many of the lessons that were taught at school. One of these was that it would do her no harm to talk to a widow, so though she dared not let her mother see her talk to Sita, she used to sit by her whenever she could get a chance to do it without being seen.

It was not a great thing for Tungi to do, for she loved to see the light steal into the frightened eyes; but if it was only another joy in Tungi's full life it was like the gate of heaven to Sita. Even to catch a passing sight of Tungi made a day a red letter day for the little widow.

Sita told Tungi all about what the woman at the well had said to her, and Tungi told her that many of those who were at school did not believe such things about widows. She told her too, that there was a better God than the ones who would treat a child as she was treated, and so she tried to comfort her little friend.

Soon Tungi had to go back to school and nine months passed before the children met again.

There had been a great contrast between them at the beginning of the nine months, but it was far greater at the end.

Tungi's eye was brighter. She had learned a great deal more, and life was interesting and glad to her. But poor Sita was sadder and more worn. Her husband's family had used her worse and worse. They had almost forgotten that she could feel, and they treated her as if she had really killed her husband.

A beautiful young widow who lived near Sita had drowned herself in a well when she found how miserable her life was after her husband's death. Sita looked into the cool water and wondered how long it would take her to die if she leapt in. Then she thought of what the woman had said a year before, and she could see herself jumping about as a little frog, and she feared that something worse even than that might happen to her, and that she might go to one of the places of punishment beyond the world altogether. So she shrank back, and tried to face the dreary round again—the hunger, the labour and the cruel pain.

RESCUED CHILD WIDOWS

Even the joy of seeing Tungi once more could scarcely raise her spirits, and the tenderness of her little friend only brought tears to her eyes. But this time Tungi had more than kindness to offer. She told Sita of Ramabai's home. It seemed impossible to Sita that she could enter there—she, whom no one wanted, and who had never been free to do what she wished. But Tungi told her that nothing could prevent her from getting into the Sharada Sadan, if she could reach it. And Sita did reach it, and what is more she reached it before all the fun and nonsense in her had been killed, and the happy years that followed healed the tiredness and the sickness of her arms and body, though they could not make her forget the darkness of her early days of widowhood.

Before Sita had heard of Ramabai's home, Tungi had said to her, "There's a better God than that." And in the Sharada Sadan Sita learned to know that God. And when she grew up a Hindu gentleman, who had also learned to know God, asked her to marry him, and Sita who had been left a widow at the age of four by the death of the "old bad man" became a happy Christian wife.

CHAPTER XV

DILAWUR KHAN AND THE KING

Far away in the north of India a little boy was born. He was trained to two things—to be a robber and to obey the Prophet Mohammed; and he learned what he was taught thoroughly, for he could steal cleverly and he was careful to pray five times a day and to fast through Ramadan. From the high hill side he watched the roads by which men crossed the country. When poor people passed along he always stayed quietly where he was, and let his sword lie by his side, though he kept his gun in his hand to be ready. But, if instead of a poor man he saw a rich trader pass, he swept down into the valley, and made the merchant a prisoner. He had hidden haunts in the hills, and he took his prisoner with him to one of them. There he kept him safely till money was sent to buy his freedom. If it was a long time before any money was sent, or if Dilawur Khan did not think that the sum that had been sent was large enough he would cut off one finger from his captive's hand and send it to his friends, to tell them that if they did not send soon it would be too late.

A price was set on Dilawur's head, and one time he was seen by some horse soldiers. They chased him, but though he ran on foot and they were on horseback they could not catch him, for he dashed into a field of tall com and lay there while they rode up and down.

At another time a government officer met him in a village, but the Englishman could not capture him there because the village was beyond the bounds of British India. But though the officer could not take him prisoner, he tried another way. He looked at the strong man before him and he felt that in spite of the wild life he was living he was a true man, so he said to him that he would give him service in the Guide Corps if he would live an honest life. But Dilawur refused the offer with scorn and said he would go on with his reckless life whatever the English said or did.

He was a faithful follower of the Prophet. Five times a day when the call for prayer rang out he bowed himself before Allah, and he kept fast each year through the month of Ramadan. Some Mohammedans have thought it a good thing even to kill those who do not worship Allah, and Dilawur Khan believed that in his life of robbery he was serving God by injuring His enemies.

But Dilawur could not forget what the officer had said to him, and the more he thought of it, the more it seemed to him that it would be better to give himself up to the English than to have them catch him as an outlaw. Besides he wished very much to get the money that had been promised to anyone who would capture him, so he found out the officer whom he had met before and asked for the reward for bringing his own head! The officer still believed that if once Dilawur gave his word he would keep it. So, instead of executing him, he allowed him to serve in the army.

One day some time after this Dilawur was in Peshawur, and as he passed through the Bazaar he saw a noisy crowd. He went up to find out what was going on, and there, to his surprise, he saw a colonel of the army speaking to those around him. As he listened he found that the colonel was speaking of the King of India, the Son of God, and he knew that he was trying to win men to believe in the foreigner's faith. Dilawur was sure that he could answer everything the colonel said, and could show the crowd that there was no truth in the religion of Christ. So he began to argue, and when he went away he took one of the colonel's books home with him in order that he might study it and prove to everyone who would listen how false it was. But when he read it, he could not prove that it was false, so he took it to three of the religious teachers of his own faith. The first one was very angry with him for reading such a book; the second told him to put it away, and to remember to pray at the set times for worship; and the third one told him that if he read such books he would lose his faith in the Prophet. This surprised him very much, because he had read the Koran, his own sacred book, for many years, and he believed in it thoroughly, and thought that any book that would make him lose his faith in the Prophet of whom the Koran told, must be a wonderful one indeed.

After some time he heard that the man who had written the book had come to Peshawur. When he heard it he said, "I would walk many miles to see that man." He went to see him and talked with him often, and from that time he began to attack the faith of those who followed the Prophet, and to urge them to prove to him the truth of the Koran. And as he thought and talked, the story of the love of Christ entered into his heart and the man who had once been a reckless robber, and who was now a brave soldier, took service also in another army and became a follower of the King.

But he had been a leader amongst the Mohammedans and they could not bear to have him leave them. They tried to kill him in many ways, and at last Dilawur was so used to attack that he challenged anyone whom he met after dark, with the words, "If you are a friend stand still!"

He served the army well, and he served Christ loyally amongst his comrades. He rose to the highest command that an Indian soldier could then hold, and he was trusted on special service. At length on one occasion a secret message had to be carried north through the mountains into Central Asia. Dilawur Khan was a true man and he knew the passes, so he was chosen to go on the dangerous errand, but ere it was finished he died amongst the snow mountains. Though he knew that he was dying, he was not afraid, but he sent a message to his officers to say that he was glad to die on duty, and a greeting to his friends. He carried the spirit of a soldier's obedience into his service of Christ. "Has He commanded?" he would ask, and if the answer was "yes," he would add, "Then that is enough for me."

CHAPTER XVI

SOOBOO

It is not only to poor and outcast girls that the sight of the King of India brings joy. There are women in that land whose lives were happy and glad before they saw Him, who yet felt, whenever they knew Him, that there was nothing that could make up to them for missing His service.

Sooboo was one of these. She was a young girl of high caste in Madras. Her father was wealthy and honoured and she still stayed with him, though she was married, because, though she had all the honour that is given to a wife, her husband would never take her to his house. She had been born on a Friday and she was one of twin children, and because of these things she would bring ill-luck to her husband's house if she entered it. She was very happy in her father's house, and she gave her time to the worship of the gods. All day long she thought of them, and planned what she could do to show her reverence for them, and to win merit by deeds of devotion.

One of her plans was to build a temple and to have within it an image of herself bowing before her god, and the image and the god were both to be made of gold. She had charge of the household gods too, and she longed to learn to read in order that she might find out for herself from the oldest Indian writings—the Vedas—what the will of the gods really was, because different priests and teachers seemed to contradict each other, and she thought that if she could get away back to the sacred books she would know better how to worship.

She tried to find some Hindu woman who would teach her. But there was not one. There were Zenana missionaries, but her friends were terribly frightened to let them near her. "They will teach you this new religion about Jesus," they said. But Sooboo was so eager to learn to read and so sure of her own faith in the Hindu gods that she said, "What they teach me about that will go in at one ear and out at the other." Sooboo had said "that." She meant the religion of the foreigners. She did not know that the Christians had a real living King whom they knew and obeyed. She thought they had just another set of rules about life and stories of gods who could be worshipped but who sat apart and had no care for the men and women who served them.

When she saw the King of India she knew Him to be her King, and the thought of Him entered deep into her heart. At first she hoped that she might stay at home and win her father and the others there to serve Christ too. His service was so wonderful to her, so different from the worship of the idols and so immensely better, that she could not believe that those she loved so well, and whom she honoured, would not serve Him too if they could only see Him.

But she did not know how fiercely her family hated the religion of the foreigner. They tried every way they could to make her yield, and when their pleading and their caresses failed, they began to ill-use her. But she did not flinch. She only thought she must be patient and wait till those whom she loved saw Jesus Christ for themselves. But one night she heard an awful thing. She heard that her people were planning to send her away to a far distant city to make her a priestess in an idol temple there. She knew too well that if they took her there, she would be forced to worship the god and to take part in rites that were hateful to her, or else to die. She had been willing to bear pain and unkindness in the hope that she might win her friends to Christ, but she could not yield to this. So one night she left her father's house and reached the home of the missionaries in safety. She would not yield to the entreaties of her friends who came to seek her, though she still loved them, and they could not force her to go back, for she was old enough to be free by law to decide for herself.

You remember the golden image of Sooboo that was being made to stand in the Hindu temple. There was another image made of Sooboo now. It was not made of gold, and it was large—as large as Sooboo herself. When it was finished it was not set up in a temple. It was laid on a stretcher like a dead body, and carried through the streets of Madras and Sooboo's father and brothers wailed out as they carried it, "Sooboo is dead!" "Sooboo is dead!" And Sooboo listened as they passed along. She heard the voices of those she loved wailing out this terrible dirge, and in her misery she covered her ears with her hands.

The image of Sooboo was burned on the funeral pyre as if it had really been Sooboo; and what followed after was even more terrible for the girl, for she heard that her mother, who had always been so much cared for, and had enjoyed the comfort and luxury of a wealthy home, and who had lived away from the sight of all except those of her own family, had taken the ashes of the image of Sooboo and had started out on foot to beg her way to the Ganges and throw the ashes on its waters. No one knew so well as Sooboo how great her mother's love for her was, when it could make her venture out into the unknown land to walk, in poverty, hundreds of miles, in order, if possible, to win forgiveness for her child. How she longed to fly to comfort her mother. But that could only be by denying her King!

Sooboo had a pilgrimage of her own to make, for she carried the devotion that had made her plan how she could best serve the gods into her service of the King. Her pilgrimage took her into the villages and the Zenanas round Madras that she might help the women of her land to see the King of India. And ever when the sight of a funeral made her think of that awful wail "Sooboo is dead," or when some aged pilgrim brought back the thought of her mother's weary steps over the burning roads of India, she turned to her own pilgrimage more eagerly, that she might hasten the time when India would know that it was life and not death to find the King, and when its peoples would crowd to Him, instead of to the Ganges.

For there is something about the King of India that makes men and women who have really seen Him feel that there is nothing so great as to serve Him, and nothing so kind as to help some one else to see Him too.

But this King of India is the King of all the world, and He still asks those who have seen Him to help Him in His kingdom. The boys and girls in India to-day could win all their land for Him if they only knew Him. But the boys and girls in Christian lands must help, for even those who are far away have their part to do. Long ago if a boy wished to be a knight he began by serving a knight. Christ the King needs many knights to ride for Him in India, to redress wrong, to save the sad and dying and the sinful; but He needs others to be servants of the knights, and each boy and girl can find something to do to help the knights of the King of India.

Printed by Libri Plureos GmbH in Hamburg,
Germany